Women in Anthropology

MAJOR WOMEN IN SCIENCE

Women in Anthropology

Shaina Indovino

Mason Crest

Mason Crest
450 Parkway Drive, Suite D
Broomall, Pennsylvania 19008
www.masoncrest.com

Printed and bound in the United States of America.

First printing
9 8 7 6 5 4 3 2 1

Series ISBN: 978-1-4222-2923-1
ISBN: 978-1-4222-2924-8
ebook ISBN: 978-1-4222-8893-1

The Library of Congress has cataloged the
hardcopy format(s) as follows:

Library of Congress Cataloging-in-Publication Data

Indovino, Shaina Carmel.
  Women in anthropology / Shaina Indovino.
      pages cm. -- (Major women in science)
  Includes index.
  ISBN 978-1-4222-2924-8 (hardcover) -- ISBN 978-1-4222-2923-1 (series) -- ISBN 978-1-4222-8893-1 (ebook)
  1. Women anthropologists--Juvenile literature. I. Title.
  GN27.I63 2014
  301.092--dc23
                        2013009811

Produced by Vestal Creative Services.
www.vestalcreative.com

Contents

Introduction

Have you wondered about how the natural world works? Are you curious about how science could help sick people get better? Do you want to learn more about our planet and universe? Are you excited to use technology to learn and share ideas? Do you want to build something new?

Scientists, engineers, and doctors are among the many types of people who think deeply about science and nature, who often have new ideas on how to improve life in our world.

We live in a remarkable time in human history. The level of understanding and rate of progress in science and technology have never been greater. Major advances in these areas include the following:

- Computer scientists and engineers are building mobile and Internet technology to help people access and share information at incredible speeds.
- Biologists and chemists are creating medicines that can target and get rid of harmful cancer cells in the body.
- Engineers are guiding robots on Mars to explore the history of water on that planet.
- Physicists are using math and experiments to estimate the age of the universe to be greater than 13 billion years old.
- Scientists and engineers are building hybrid cars that can be better for our environment.

Scientists are interested in discovering and understanding key principles in nature, including biological, chemical, mathematical, and physical aspects of our world. Scientists observe, measure, and experiment in a systematic way in order to test and improve their understanding. Engineers focus on applying scientific knowledge and math to find creative solutions for technical problems and to develop real products for people to use. There are many types of engineering, including computer, electrical, mechanical, civil, chemical, and biomedical engineering. Some people have also found that studying science or engineering can help them succeed in other professions such as law, business, and medicine.

Both women and men can be successful in science and engineering. This book series highlights women leaders who have made significant contributions across many scientific fields, including chemistry, medicine, anthropology, engineering, and physics. Historically, women have faced barriers to training and building careers in science,

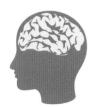

which makes some of these stories even more amazing. While not all barriers have been overcome, our society has made tremendous progress in educating and advancing women in science. Today, there are schools, organizations, and resources to enable women to pursue careers as scientists or engineers at the highest levels of achievement and leadership.

The goals of this series are to help you:

1. Learn about women scientists, engineers, doctors, and inventors who have made a major impact in science and our society
2. Understand different types of science and engineering
3. Explore science and math in school and real life

You can do a lot of things to learn more about science, math, and engineering. Explore topics in books or online, take a class at school, go to science camp, or do experiments at home. More important, talk to a real scientist! Call or e-mail your local college to find students and professors. They would love to meet with you. Ask your doctors about their education and training. Or you can check out these helpful resources:

- *Nova* has very cool videos about science, including profiles on real-life women scientists and engineers: www.pbs.org/wgbh/nova.
- *National Geographic* has excellent photos and stories to inspire people to care about the planet: science.nationalgeographic.com/science.
- Here are examples of online courses for students, of which many are free to use:
    1. Massachusetts Institute of Technology (MIT) OpenCourseWare highlights for high school: http://ocw.mit.edu/high-school
    2. Khan Academy tutorials and courses: www.khanacademy.org.
    3. Stanford University Online, featuring video courses and programs for middle and high school students: online.stanford.edu.

Other skills will become important as you get older. Build strong communication skills, such as asking questions and sharing your ideas in class. Ask for advice or help when needed from your teachers, mentors, tutors, or classmates. Be curious and resilient: learn from your successes and mistakes. The best scientists do.

Learning science and math is one of the most important things that you can do in school. Knowledge and experience in these areas will teach you how to think and how the world works and can provide you with many adventures and paths in life. I hope you will explore science—you could make a difference in this world.

Ann Lee-Karlon, PhD
President
Association for Women in Science
San Francisco, California

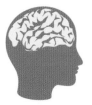

1

What Does It Take to Be an Anthropologist?

Where do humans come from? How has human society changed over time? Why are cultures from around the world so different from your own? If you ever find yourself asking these questions, you might be interested in becoming an anthropologist!

An anthropologist is a person who studies anthropology—which means the "science of humanity." It's a very broad field. There are many different types of anthropologists in the world. Some anthropologists examine the human body and how it has evolved over time. Other anthropologists are more interested in culture or the **artifacts** left behind by societies of the past.

Being an anthropologist is a rewarding career—but becoming one is not easy. Most anthropologists spend a very long time in school. When an anthropologist finishes school, she may already be considered an expert in her field. However, a good anthropologist is always looking to learn more.

When the field of anthropology first began, most anthropologists were men. At the time, it was easier for a man to receive the education he needed to become a scientist. Unlike men, very few women went to college. This made scientists who were women extremely rare. Even if a woman did manage to get the education she needed, she faced even more challenges. People often didn't accept that she was as intelligent as the men in her field. They didn't think she could do as good a job as a man could. Sometimes, they even felt she was immoral for not staying in the home, taking care of a family.

The first female anthropologists were forced to prove their capabilities in order to be taken seriously. These brave women paved the road for the female anthropologists of the future. Fortunately, it is now much easier for women to become anthropologists today.

Why Be an Anthropologist?

Would you rather read a history book about the people of South America or take a trip there yourself? Some scientists, known as field scientists, choose to go out into the world to experience what they are studying firsthand. They believe that they can learn more this way than by sitting behind a desk.

The way an anthropologist does her research depends on what she wishes to study. An archaeologist might spend years in Egypt digging up ancient tombs. A biological anthropologist might go deep into the jungle to study our primate relatives in their natural habitat. A cultural anthropologist may travel to a village in rural China to speak with the people there. Not all anthropologists travel far, but they all immerse themselves fully in whatever they are studying.

Being an anthropologist is more than just a job; it is a way of life. It is not uncommon to spend years in a foreign area doing your research. Anthropologists must be passionate about what they do.

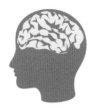

An anthropologist often studies bones to discover clues about how ancient people lived. Teeth and skulls can reveal a lot about an ancient people's lifestyle.

Education

If you want to be an anthropologist, you will first need a good education. Most anthropologists spend at least six to eight years in school after graduating high school.

Many universities offer four-year degrees in anthropology. Some colleges will even offer **specializations** within the field. These may include biological anthropology, cultural anthropology, or archaeology. If you already know the specific field you would like to study, start early! While you are still in school, you will want to learn all you can from your professors both inside and outside of the classroom.

After college, you will need to move on to graduate school. In order to get into graduate school, you will need great grades! Graduate school degrees usually take about two to ten years to complete. Many anthropologists earn a doctorate

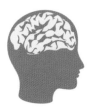

These artifacts from an ancient Native American culture allow anthropologists to learn more about prehistoric human societies.

degree in their specific area of study. While you earn a graduate degree, you will spend even more time with your professors.

The road to becoming an anthropologist does not stop with college. Anthropologists never stop learning. You should try to research and travel as much as you can after you graduate. Publishing your discoveries is an important way to become recognized and respected in the scientific community.

Character

Two of the most important qualities found in any anthropologist are **dedication** and curiosity. A good anthropologist never stops asking questions and is always eager to learn more.

An anthropologist must also be open-minded. This is because what we understand about the world is constantly changing. Our knowledge of the past is limited. This might make some anthropologists feel like they are trying to solve a puzzle without having all of the pieces. This can be frustrating at first. Once the puzzle is solved and the answer is found, it can be very rewarding.

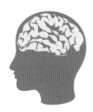

Like all scientists, anthropologists need to be objective. To be objective means to base your decisions on facts alone. You might think what one foreign culture does is odd, for example, but if you're objective, you'll remember that what we do might be considered odd to them. The best anthropologists try their best to help the world see that we are all connected in one way or another. After all, we are all humans, and anthropology is the study of humanity.

Women are just as likely to have these qualities as men are. Today, more women are seizing the opportunity to become anthropologists.

Words to Know

Artifacts: objects made by human beings, usually of historical or cultural interest.
Specializations: specific areas of research.
Dedication: commitment to something.

Find Out More

American Anthropological Association: "Resources For Students"
www.aaanet.org/resources/students

Boston University: "Why Major in Anthropology?"
www.bu.edu/anthrop/undergraduate/why-major-in-anthropology

Strang, Veronica. *What Anthropologists Do.* Oxford, UK: Berg, 2009.

Thomas, Peggy. *Talking Bones: The Science of Forensic Anthropology.* New York: Facts on File, 2008.

Sokanu: "Anthropologist"
www.sokanu.com/careers/anthropologist

Ruth Benedict:
Achievement Against the Odds

One of the most important qualities an anthropologist can have is open-mindedness. Ruth Benedict was as open-minded as she could possibly be for her time. When she was born in 1887, female scientists were not common. In fact, a woman attending college was a rare sight. Many women were looked down upon just for seeking a higher education. Against all odds, Ruth Benedict became one of the first and most famous female anthropologists.

Ruth Benedict did not always know she would be an anthropologist. When she graduated from Vassar College, she left with a degree in English. Little did she know that she was already thinking like an anthropologist from an early age.

When Ruth was a young girl, her father died of an unknown disease. Her mother became overcome with grief, which puzzled young Ruth. Instead of dismissing it, Ruth began to question why. Why were some people nearly destroyed by grief while others were able to accept it? Even at a young age, Ruth understood that each event affected people differently. She was also given a unique perspective of the world when she became partially deaf as a result of a childhood illness.

Poetry was one of Ruth's first **passions**. Then she fell in love with anthropology after taking a class with one of Franz Boas' students. Once she began studying with Franz Boas directly, she knew what her life calling would be. At this time, she met Margaret Mead, who would become a lifelong friend. The two formed a unique friendship based on the fact that they were both female anthropologists, something that was so rare at the time.

Anthropology at a Distance

Anthropologists don't only help us understand the past. They can help us understand the present, too. Many cultural anthropologists try to understand as much as they can about a culture by visiting the area and interviewing members of that society. This is very effective because it allows the anthropologist to have a firsthand experience. Unfortunately, this isn't always possible. During World War II, the Allied Forces wanted to learn as much as they could about the Axis Powers without actually traveling to Germany or Japan. This is where Ruth Benedict came in. She studied everything she could about Japan without physically going there. Some of her sources included literature, newspaper clippings, and films. Her discoveries were published in one of her most famous books, *The Chrysanthemum and the Sword*, after World War II was over.

Franz Boas inspired Ruth to become an anthropologist.

One of her books, *Patterns of Culture*, made Ruth become a well-respected anthropologist. In it, Ruth introduced the idea that each culture is dominated by certain personality traits. These personality traits continue on as a pattern through the generations of each culture. She examined different Native American tribes for her study. The ideas presented in this book were so **revolutionary** at the time that some anthropology courses still require students to read *Patterns of Culture*.

In addition to her academic work, Ruth fought for equality for all, using arguments founded in anthropology. She stated that although a person may look different, we all have the potential to be equally intelligent. Like Margaret Mead, another famous woman anthropologist, Ruth Benedict argued that our environment has more influence on who we become than our genes do. Intelligence is more likely to be determined by income and education rather than what **ethnicity** someone is.

Ruth Benedict's message resonated with women who were seeking liberation. Ruth insisted that all people are born equal. Her example as a female scientist also showed women that they could do anything they set their minds to. Over the next few decades, women looked to Ruth as an inspiration as they fought for equal rights.

Ruth Benedict taught at Columbia University until her death in 1948. She was known as a shy but passionate professor who was able to clearly explain her ideas to her students. And her ideas helped changed the world for the women who came after her!

Words to Know

Passions: extreme enthusiasms for.
Revolutionary: causing a complete and dramatic change.
Ethnicity: a social identity associated with belonging to a group that shares cultural or historical ties.

Find Out More

Benedict, Ruth. *Patterns of Culture*. Boston: Houghton Mifflin, 2005.

Benedict, Ruth. *The Chrysanthemum and the Sword: Patterns of Japanese Culture*. Boston: Houghton Mifflin, 2005.

Mead, Margaret. *Ruth Benedict: A Humanist in Anthropology*. New York: Columbia University Press, 2005.

Vassar Encyclopedia: "Ruth Benedict." vcencyclopedia.vassar.edu/alumni/ruth-benedict.html

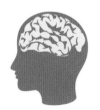

Zora Neale Hurston:
Author & Anthropologist

Some anthropologists are born into a situation that forces them to examine cultural differences from an early age. This was certainly the case with Zora Neale Hurston. Unlike most anthropologists, Zora was both a woman and an African American. This gave her a unique perspective in her line of work.

Zora was born on January 7, 1891. She grew up in the town of Eatonville, Florida, where almost every single person was of African American descent. Because the entire town was black, members of that community were free to express themselves as they pleased without judgment or restriction. With no whites around, they didn't have to encounter prejudice and discrimination until they left town. These early years caused Zora to greatly appreciate her heritage. This was where her creative and curious nature began to bloom.

As she went off into the world, Zora noticed key differences between the cultures of different ethnic groups. Because she appreciated her own culture so much, she understood the importance of preserving the cultures of others. She opposed **integration** for this reason. In Zora's opinion, it was best to keep different cultures separate so that they did not lose their sense of identity.

Although she enjoyed her life at home, Zora yearned to receive a proper education. She worked on the road as a maid to the lead singer of a traveling troupe and eventually ended up in the northeastern United States. At the age of twenty-six, she wanted to enroll in a public high school. Unfortunately, her age restricted her, because at her age, her education would no longer be free. Zora was so desperate to go to high school that she lied about her year of birth, saying it was actually ten years later. From that point forward, she swore she was born in the year 1901 for legal reasons. This showed that she was a woman that wasn't going to let anything stand in her way!

Zora Hurston was eventually offered a scholarship to Columbia University, where a black woman receiving a higher education was a rare sight. Fortunately, Zora found a place in the university where she belonged. She worked alongside many well-known anthropologists, including Franz Boas, Ruth Benedict, and Margaret Mead.

In a generation where most people thought a black woman had little to offer the world, Zora Hurston proved them wrong.

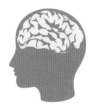

As an anthropologist, Zora enjoyed researching the cultures of foreign locations, including the Caribbean, Jamaica, Haiti, and the Honduras. Traveling and learning about the world was one of her passions. The islands off the coast of Florida were the areas she chose to make her specialty. One of her most famous works, *Tell My Horse*, explores the voodoo practices and beliefs in Haiti and Jamaica.

In addition to anthropology, Zora was also interested in literature. Throughout her lifetime, she wrote many stories based on her own life, in addition to papers discussing what she discovered on her travels. Her experience as a writer allowed her to befriend other well-known writers, including Langston Hughes. One of her most famous stories is the novel, *Their Eyes Were Watching God*. The novel became so popular that a movie based on it was released in 2005.

Toward the end of her life, Zora gained recognition for her contributions to both anthropology and literature. Those who remember her say she was a charming, intelligent woman who was always the "life of the party." Unfortunately, she did not earn a lot of money in life and was buried in an unmarked grave. Today, though, many people have been touched by her **legacy**. Zora remains an inspiration to anthropologists, writers, travelers, African Americans, and women. An annual festival is held in her hometown of Eatonville to celebrate her life.

Words to Know

Integration: mixing of people who were previously kept apart.

Legacy: the ideas or objects left behind by someone who has died, and which continue to influence others.

Find Out More

Boyd, Valerie. *Wrapped in Rainbows: The Life of Zora Neale Hurston*. New York: Scribner, 2004.

Zora Neale Hurston: "The Official Website of Zora Neale Hurston"
www.zoranealehurston.com

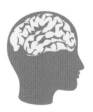

Camilla Hildegarde Wedgwood:

Anthropologist & Educator

Many female anthropologists rose above the odds to become successful and respected. Not everyone made an active effort to change these odds for other women, however. After gaining the respect of her **peers** as an anthropologist, Camilla Hildegarde Wedgwood devoted her life to helping other women achieve a proper education. Because of her, today's young female scientists have an easier time in today's academic world.

Camilla Wedgwood was born on March 25, 1901 in Barlaston, England. Her parents separated and eventually divorced when she was a child. In the early 1900s, divorce was not as common as it is today, so the fact that her parents divorced may have been one of the reasons Camilla became interested in the differences between cultures.

Camilla studied how the women of New Guinea lived by living with them and following their customs.

The Wedgwood name was well known at the time because of the fine pottery their company produced. This may have made it easier for Camilla to obtain an education. While in school, Camilla studied English, anthropology, and archaeology.

During this time, she studied under Alfred Court Haddon, a respected anthropologist. After graduating, Haddon asked Camilla to edit the manuscript of *Malekula: A Vanishing People in the New Hebrides* by Arthur Bernard Deacon.

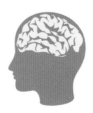

Bernard Deacon was another one of Alfred Haddon's students who had died in 1927. This experience helped establish Camilla in her field.

Like other anthropologists, Camilla spent much of her early career teaching and traveling. The first place she taught was a school she had attended, Bedford College in England. She then divided her time between two continents. While abroad, she taught at the University of Sydney in Australia and the University of Cape Town in South Africa, two locations that were very far apart from each other. The native cultures of these two areas were very different, especially when compared to Camilla's homeland.

When she finally returned to England, she was offered the opportunity of a lifetime. In 1932, she was given money by the Australian Research Council to conduct field research on Manam Island in New Guinea. Very little was known about the inhabitants of the island at this time. Most of the **Western** world had assumed they were uncivilized. Camilla's study would change this opinion forever.

Getting Involved

Some cultural anthropologists think the best way to understand a culture is to become part of it. Camilla Wedgwood was one of these anthropologists. During her research on the island of Manam, she did her best to follow the customs of the people there. This included eating and preparing food like them and participating in the rituals of their culture. By the end of her stay, she was very friendly with the people of Manam despite her very different upbringing. Camilla's experiences give us an in-depth look at how those people lived that would not have been possible if she had merely observed them as an outsider.

Unlike some other anthropologists before her, Camilla's research focused mainly on women and children. She believed that the women of Manam were more equal to the males of Manam than the women of Western nations. Accord-

Camilla Hildegarde Wedgwood 25

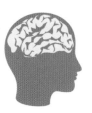

ing to her, it was the advances of the Western world that caused women to be dependent on men. **Primitive** cultures, she argued, had more equality for this reason. This goes against what other anthropologists have claimed, and is still debated today.

Camilla's experiences in New Guinea opened up other opportunities for her. By this time, she was known as a talented researcher, and other communities sought her out to conduct similar research. The government of Nauru, having heard of her previous success in the Pacific, asked her to study their culture. (Like Manam, Nauru is located in the Pacific Ocean.) The purpose of this research was to revive the native Nauru culture before it was lost to history. Camilla was eager to take on this task.

Her time in Nauru gained her even more popularity. Following her study there, she returned to the University of Sydney, where she became the principal of the Women's College. As the acting leader and female role model of the school, she encouraged culture and growth among the students there.

Camilla worked with the government of Nairu to protect the native culture. This image shows a school where the children of Nairu could learn about their own culture as well as the larger world.

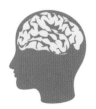

Later in life, Camilla became increasingly interested in the education of young women. She felt that women were not given equal opportunities. Camilla made it her personal mission to change that, while also encouraging others to do the same. Many of her lectures as a staff member of the School of Pacific Administration were about the importance of education. Women all around the world, but especially in Australia, have female scientists like Camilla Wedgwood to thank for the opportunities women now have.

Words to Know

Peers: people who are of equal standing in a group because they are the same age, rank, or have the same knowledge.

Western: referring to parts of the world heavily influenced by European thought, including Europe, North America, and Australia.

Primitive: less advanced; referring to groups of people who have limited technology and simpler social structures.

Find Out More

Wetherell, David, and Charlotte Carr-Gregg. *Camilla: C.H. Wedgwood, 1901–1955, a Life*. Kensington, N.S.W.: New South Wales University Press, 2000.

Webster University: "Camilla Hildegard Wedgwood"
www2.webster.edu/~woolflm/camillawedgewood.html

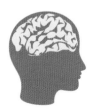

5

Margaret Mead: Understanding the South Pacific

Have you ever heard someone discuss the difference between "nature" and "nurture"? They are two words to describe how we become who we are. A person who believes in "nature" thinks we are born with the personality we will have in life. We're the way we are because it's our nature to be that way! They might also say personality and beliefs are **genetic**. A person who believes in "nurture" thinks we develop our personality and beliefs over time. We learn them from the people we grow up around. These might include our parents, grandparents, teachers, and friends. People who believe in "nurture" would say we're also shaped by our environment (whether we live in the city or in the country, for example, or in the United States or Kenya) and by the society in which we live. Many people now believe both nature and nurture influence our personalities, health, and lives in different ways.

Margaret Mead studied people—but she also studied information from books. As an anthropologist, her work built on research done by earlier anthropologists. Then she added to that research by writing books of her own.

During Margaret Mead's time, many people believed in "nature"—that we are born with our personality traits. Margaret believed that we develop our beliefs over time, and she did research to show the effects of nurture on human thinking and development.

Margaret was born on December 16, 1901, right at the turn of the century. She was the oldest of five children. Both of her parents were **progressive** thinkers. They believed the problems of the world could be fixed by thinking about them in a **social context**. When Margaret was a little girl, her mother recorded observations about her daughter in a diary. A few of these notes described Margaret as affectionate, wishing to be helpful, having great determination and **perseverance**, and continually asking questions. Margaret didn't change much as she got older!

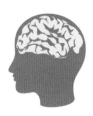

Choosing a Specialization

Many anthropologists choose to become an expert in one geographical area. In Margaret's case, she chose the South Pacific Islands. Choosing one location as your area of study has a few advantages. First, it allows an anthropologist to learn a lot about one culture. Second, it allows anthropologists to compare two close cultures in order to find what makes them similar and what makes them different. Finally, it allows an anthropologist to stay in one place for a long time. By staying in one geographic location, an anthropologist can truly get to know what she is studying. She can interview the people of the area, examine the living conditions, and experience the climate.

Even from a very young age, Margaret was already thinking like a scientist. When her brother and sisters were still babies, Margaret's grandmother encouraged Margaret to observe them. Margaret wrote down what she learned. She continued to keep accounts of her experiences throughout life. The young Margaret spent a lot of time outdoors learning about natural history and botany. (No wonder she went on to become a **curator** at the American Museum of Natural History in New York City!)

When Margaret first went to college, she was unhappy. After a year at the college her father had attended, she transferred to Barnard College, an all-women's college in New York City. Here she met Franz Boas, a well-respected anthropologist. Today, he is often called the Father of American anthropology. After taking a class with him, Margaret discovered her love for the field of anthropology. She also became very close with Ruth Benedict, one of Franz Boas' teaching assistants.

After earning her undergraduate degree, Margaret went on to earn a PhD. During this time, she traveled a lot. She was mainly interested in the cultures of the South Pacific. One of her most famous works, *Coming of Age in Samoa*, is based on her time and research there. The book outlines her discovery that

the children of different South Pacific groups behaved very differently from one another. This suggested that children learn their role within society from their surroundings and not from their **genes**. Following the publication of this book, Margaret became one of the most famous anthropologists of her time.

Although many people found Margaret's book to be eye-opening, she upset many others. Some people did not believe her findings. Others were upset by the practices of Samoan culture because they believed them to be wrong. According to Margaret's research, a Samoan woman spent time with many men before getting married. This went against the Western belief that a woman should be with only one man and she should be married to him for her entire life. Margaret's works remind us that a good anthropologist must be willing to look at the world through another culture's perspective.

As Margaret grew older, she became more interested in the culture of the United States and chose to do her research at home. She went on to teach at many different universities within the United States. These included Columbia University, New York University, and Yale University. She even founded the **urban anthropology** department at New York University. In addition to teaching, she became a leader in many important anthropological organizations. One of these was the American Anthropological Association. In 1971, much of her work was displayed at the Museum of Natural History, where she was a curator throughout much of her young adult life. Because the museum is so large and well known, this was a great honor for her.

On a personal level, Margaret also lived a very different life from those around her. She married and divorced a total of three times. This was very uncommon in her day. She also chose to keep her maiden name (Mead) when she was married, even though at the time, most women took their spouses' last names. Margaret was not afraid to be different!

Margaret Mead died on November 15, 1978, at the age of seventy-six. A year later, President Jimmy Carter awarded her the Presidential Medal of Freedom to honor her for her contributions to anthropology and science. Margaret Mead remains an inspiration and example for all young anthropologists. She showed them that they could dare to be different!

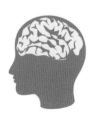

Words to Know

Genetic: passed down from parents to children through DNA.

Progressive: favoring social reform and embracing changes and new ideas.

Social context: the cultural ideas, beliefs, and values a person grows up with.

Perseverance: the willingness to keep going despite hardship.

Curator: a person who takes care of a museum collection.

Genes: the parts of DNA that allow living things to pass on traits to their children.

Urban anthropology: the study of people living in cities.

Find Out More

Library of Congress: "Margaret Mead: Human Nature and the Power of Culture"
www.loc.gov/exhibits/mead

Mead, Margaret. *Blackberry Winter: My Earlier Years*. New York: Kodansha International, 1995.

Mead, Margaret. *Coming of Age in Samoa*. New York: Perennial, 2001.

Webster University: "Margaret Mead, 1901–1978"
www2.webster.edu/~woolflm/margaretmead.html

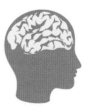

6

Erika Bourguignon:
Learning from the Holocaust

All anthropologists are interested in humanity. Erika Bourguignon was no different. What most interested her, however, was the human mind and how it has changed over time. The field that studies this question is known as psychological anthropology. Throughout her life, Erika conducted many studies centered around this interest. As a female anthropologist, she also recognized the importance of women throughout history. Some of her studies centered around women of both other cultures and our own.

Erika was born in 1924 in Vienna, Austria. Little is known about her life as a child. She came to the United States in 1939 and received her bachelor's degree from Queens College in New York, and at this time she found a passion for anthropology. She later earned her PhD from Northwestern University.

Looking to the Past

Many anthropologists understand the importance of those who came before them. After all, the field of anthropology would not be where it is today without the studies of the past. In addition to her own studies, Erika Bourguignon took it upon herself to write about the anthropologists of the past. Some of the people she wrote about shared her interests. George Devereux, one of her subjects, was interested in Native Americans, just as she was.

In her early career, Erika traveled to other countries. One of these was Haiti. During her stay in Haiti, she met her future husband, a Belgian artist named Paul-Henri Bourguignon. One of her papers, "Haiti and the Art of Paul-Henri Bourguignon," describes their experiences together. While in Haiti, Erika observed the rituals and cultures of the native people. In addition to studying the Haitian culture, she also was interested in the Native Americans, most specifically the Chippewa Indians in Wisconsin.

One of Erika's major discoveries was that many religions practice some form of an **altered state of consciousness**. Although the names and methods differ, the effects are similar. Erika wanted to find out why.

Throughout her studies, Erika learned that many religions believe in possession, that the human body can be taken over by an outside force. In certain religions, the possessor is a foreign spirit. In her work entitled *Possession*, she explains that the concept is ancient and surprisingly common. About 70 percent of sample societies believe in possession, while as much as 90 percent believe in a trance-like state of altered consciousness. She believed that the intersection between the physical body and the mind can be found within altered consciousness.

Another of Erika's interests was how we think about events of the past. The Jewish Holocaust was one of the traumatic events she examined. The fact that she was born in Austria no doubt influenced her interest in the subject.

Some people believe we should remember all we can about the Holocaust so that it doesn't happen again. Others try to **suppress** the memory because it is too painful to think about. In her paper, "Memory in an Amnesic World: Holocaust, Exile, and the Return of the Suppressed," Erika examined the trend of suppressing events that are too hard to think about. She also advised that we look toward other cultures for how they handle similar experiences.

Much of Erika's later career centered around teaching. She began teaching at the University of Ohio in 1949, and she continued teaching there for more than forty years, eventually becoming the chair of the Department of Anthropology. The courses she taught focused on African, Caribbean, and Latin American culture. She was honored with an Alumni Distinguished Scholar Award from the university where she worked.

Erika Bourguignon broke important new ground in field of anthropology. Many of the areas she studied had rarely if ever been studied before. Her life proves to us that it is okay to branch out into uncharted territory, even if no one else has been there before.

Words to Know

Altered state of consciousness: a way of being conscious that is very different from normal daily consciousness, often induced by drugs.
Suppress: to prevent from happening.

Find Out More

Erika Bourguignon: An Interview
onlinelibrary.wiley.com/doi/10.1525/ac.1999.10.2-3.50/abstract

Psychology Today. "What Is Psychological Anthropology?"
www.psychologytoday.com/blog/sex-drugs-and-boredom/200909/what-is-psychological-anthropology

7

Jane Goodall: Friend of the Chimpanzees

Many anthropologists believe that in order to better understand ourselves, we must first look at where we came from. Jane Goodall took this to a whole new level when she chose to spend decades studying chimpanzees in the wild. In addition to being an anthropologist, Jane was a primatologist. Primatologists study primates. (Chimpanzees are just one example of a primate.) Many scientists believe that the human species has evolved from primates. Primatologists like Jane believe we can learn more about our own species by studying the primates.

Does an Anthropologist Need to Go to College?

Unlike many famous anthropologists of her time, Jane did not attend college before conducting her field research. Later in her career, other scientists would criticize her lack of formal education. This, in addition to being a woman, made it difficult for Jane to be taken seriously at first. Over time, Jane was able to prove herself. In fact, her lack of a formal education may have been part of why she was so successful. Jane was able to "think outside the box" and bring new perspectives to the field of anthropology. Today, she is well-respected for her methods.

Jane Goodall was born on April 3, 1934, in London. She became a lover of animals early on and dreamed of one day living among the animals in the wild. As a child, her two favorite books were *Tarzan* and *Dr. Dolittle*, two books with heroes that spend their time surrounded by animals in their natural habitats. She enjoyed spending time outside in nature, making observations and drawing sketches of the wildlife there.

As a young adult, Jane took a trip to Africa. One of her first stops was Kenya, where she visited a childhood friend. There she met Louis Leakey, a Kenyan archaeologist. He was so impressed with her enthusiasm and knowledge about animals that he invited her to assist him with his work. Like Jane, Louis Leakey had an incredible interest in chimpanzees because they were known as one of the most intelligent primates.

Very little was known about the chimpanzees' way of life at the time. Louis Leakey wanted to learn more about them, but there was one problem: chimpanzees were known to be very shy creatures. Because of this, humans couldn't observe chimpanzees' habitat without frightening them. In order for scientists to successfully observe chimps in the wild, they would need to spend a lot of time

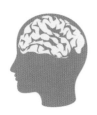

Jane Goodall has never stopped working to help people understand chimpanzees. Today, the Jane Goodall Institute works to both educate people about great apes and protect these animals. These young chimpanzees live at Jane's Tchimpounga Chimpanzee Rehabilitation Center in the Republic of Congo. The center gives traumatized orphan chimpanzees, who are often sick, malnourished, and close to death, a second chance at a happy life.

with them in order to earn their trust. Louis Leakey believed that Jane would be the perfect person to take on this task—and she was very eager to try!

When Jane first began observing the chimps of Tanzania, she found it hard not to be discouraged. She could not see them well without binoculars, and if she went too close, they would run away. Any other scientist might have given up, but not Jane! She was persistent. Jane knew that one day all of her hard work would eventually pay off.

Eventually, Jane found a hill where she was able to observe the chimps without scaring them away. Over time, she was able to slowly move closer as the chimpanzees grew more comfortable with her presence. From that point forward, she made some amazing discoveries. Before Jane's work, scientists believed that chimpanzees were vegetarians, that they did not eat meat. During Jane's studies, she witnessed several chimpanzees eating small animals.

She also witnessed chimpanzees using simple tools, something many anthropologists had thought was unique to humans. Chimpanzees would use twigs to fish for termites and other insects within the holes of trees. When the chimps pulled the twigs out, they would eat the delicious meal that was on the end of them.

Unlike other scientists, Jane believed she needed to understand chimps on a personal level. Instead of numbering the chimpanzees like other anthropologists might have done, she gave them personal names, like David Greybeard, Goliath,

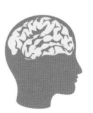

Mike, and Humphrey. This was unheard of at the time and very **controversial**. Jane quickly learned that each chimpanzee had a very unique personality, making them even more similar to humans than she originally thought.

Jane spent many years with the chimpanzees before finally concluding her study. She is one of the few people to earn a PhD from Cambridge University without having earned a bachelor's degree first. Today, she continues to travel and educate those around her about the importance of preserving primate society and learning all we can from it. Gombe Stream National Park, where she conducted her study, is still a very famous site. Among many other honors, Jane Goodall was recognized as a UN Messenger of Peace in 2002.

Jane's experiences remind us that you do not need to follow the typical path of becoming an anthropologist. And you don't have to be a man to prove yourself!

Words to Know
Controversial: causing widespread disagreement.

Find Out More
Biography.com: "Jane Goodall"
www.biography.com/people/jane-goodall-9542363

Edwards, Roberta. *Who Is Jane Goodall?* New York: Grosset & Dunlap, 2012.

Goodall, Jane. *In the Shadow of Man*. Boston: Mariner, 2009.

Goodall, Jane, and Dale Peterson. *Africa in My Blood: An Autobiography in Letters: The Early Years*. Boston: Houghton Mifflin, 2001.

The Jane Goodall Institute
www.janegoodall.org

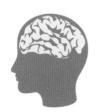

8

Dian Fossey: Living with Gorillas

S ometimes, a scientist becomes very close to what they are studying. This is what happened with Dian Fossey. When she first began studying the apes of Africa, she did so as a scientist. Over time, she grew very passionate about the apes she was studying and fought hard to protect them. If you spend decades surrounded by the same group of animals, they will eventually feel like family! By the end of her life, she was known both for her scientific discoveries and her love for the animals to which she had devoted her life.

Dian Fossey was born on January 16, 1932. Her love for animals can be traced back to when she began horseback riding lessons as a child. She originally took business courses in college, but then she decided to follow her passion for animals and enrolled in a pre-veterinary course. Unfortunately, she did not do well in all her classes, and she was forced to change majors. Instead, Dian became an **occupational therapist**. Even though she wasn't helping animals, she still found an outlet for her **compassionate** nature.

Before long, though, she had the opportunity to travel to Africa. While on a seven-week visit to Africa, she met Louis Leakey, the same anthropologist who had helped Jane Goodall get started. Dian talked with him about their mutual interest in apes before she returned home. Louis Leakey and Dian then met again several years later in Louisville, Kentucky, where she was living at the time. He remembered her interest in gorillas and encouraged her to travel back to Africa to research them.

Because of her love for animals and the outdoors, Dian accepted Louis Leakey's proposal and prepared to go back to Africa. Like Jane Goodall when she started out, Dian had almost no formal education in animals or animal behavioral research. She simply loved animals and was willing to endure the harsh conditions of the Congo to observe primates in the wild.

Although Jane Goodall was already researching chimpanzees, gorillas and chimpanzees are not the same. They are two different species with very different habitats, behaviors, and social structures. What Dian learned from the gorillas in the Congo and Rwanda was very different from what Jane learned from the chimps of Tanzania.

Learning from the Experts

Every scientist needs to start somewhere. Sometimes, it is best to ask those that came before you for advice. In Dian's case, she was able to learn from a study that was very similar to her own. Before Dian Fossey began her own research, she met with Jane Goodall. At the time, Jane Goodall was observing the chimpanzees in Tanzania. Dian Fossey saw this as a perfect opportunity to learn all she could before attempting to watch the wild apes of the Congo, and later Rwanda.

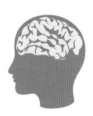

Dian studied gorillas and learned from them by living among them. They learned to trust her, allowing her to learn their secrets.

Gorillas are extremely large. Because of this, some people might think that they are very aggressive and violent. One of Dian's most important discoveries was that this simply isn't true. Gorillas are sometimes referred to as "gentle giants" because they are very social and seldom violent. Dian observed that gorillas also have individual personalities.

Like other primates, however, you must earn a gorilla's trust before it will let you close enough to it to study it. Dian did this by imitating the behavior of a gorilla. She grunted like a gorilla and even ate the same food as the gorillas. Eventually, the gorillas were completely comfortable with her presence. This allowed her to observe their complex social structure and even participate in it. Dian quickly learned that these unique creatures have a lot to teach us about our own origins as human beings.

Unfortunately, few gorillas are left in the wild. One of the biggest reasons for this is poaching. Poachers hunt wild gorillas for their skin and fur. Soon after be-

Siguourney Weaver played Dian Fossey in the 1988 movie *Gorillas in the Mist.*

ginning her research, Dian focused her attention on protecting the animals she had grown to understand and love. Poachers became her enemy, which caused a lot of tension between her and the locals of Rwanda.

Later in her life, Dian earned a PhD and taught at Cornell University. She died at her camp in Rwanda doing what she loved most: spending time with the gorillas and protecting them. She is remembered as a primatologist who wasn't afraid to stand up for what she believed. Her book, *Gorillas in the Mist,* recounts her life among the gorillas. It was later made into a very successful film by the same name.

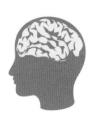

Words to Know

Occupational therapist: a person who helps others with disabilities learn how to live normal, independent physical and emotional lives.

Compassionate: feeling or showing sympathy and concern for others.

Find Out More

Fossey, Dian. *Gorillas in the Mist*. Boston: Houghton Mifflin, 1983.

Weber, William, and Amy Vedder. *In the Kingdom of Gorillas: Fragile Species in a Dangerous Land*. New York: Simon & Schuster, 2002.

De, La Bédoyère, Camilla., and Dian Fossey. *No One Loved Gorillas More: Dian Fossey, Letters from the Mist*. Washington, D.C.: National Geographic, 2005.

PBS. "The Gorilla King: More on Dian Fossey and Her Research" www.pbs.org/wnet/nature/episodes/the-gorilla-king/more-on-dian-fossey-and-her-research/737

9

Galina Vasilievna Starovoitova:

Anthropologist & Politician

Unlike some anthropologists, Galina Vasilievna Starovoitova became very politically active. Most anthropologists published their findings in books and papers. Galina didn't think this was enough. She wanted to make a difference in a very big way, so she became a politician. Her background in anthropology allowed her to bring a unique perspective to lawmaking.

Galina was born on May 17, 1946, in Russia. Although she grew up in the mountains, far away from any city, she was determined to have an education. She earned her undergraduate degree and quickly moved on to graduate school, where she earned a masters degree in social psychology and eventually a PhD in social anthropology.

Galina was most interested in the many different ethnic groups that existed in Russia. She was fascinated by how different groups interacted, but she was also upset by the unfair treatment that some groups received. She spent many years working as an ethnographer and psychologist. During this time, she published her findings for others to read.

Although Galina is best known as a politician, she did not become politically active until late in life. In fact, she didn't officially enter the political field until 1989. Once there, she did her best to make a difference with her newfound influence.

If Galina had thought being a female scientist was hard, she soon found that being a female politician was even harder! One of her greatest causes was the protection of the Armenian people, an ethnic minority found in Russia. Galina believed strongly in reform: she insisted that the government should be drastically changed. She supported democracy and rejected communism. Because communism was very popular at the time, her opinions gained her many enemies. Those that appreciated her perspective became her friends.

Galina Starovoitova's opinions were clearly influenced by her background in anthropology. She was an outspoken **advocate** for human rights, believing that all people should be treated equally. She spent the remainder of her life dedicated to this cause. In 1996, she became the first Russian woman to run for president. Although she did not win, she did not give up her fight to apply her knowledge of anthropology to the world of politics.

Throughout her political career, Galina also traveled around the world, acting as an advisor to foreign nations. At one point, she was a professor in the United States. Her teaching focused on the importance of ethics, the fair treatment of all human beings.

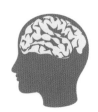

Armenia

One of the subjects Galina felt most passionate about was the treatment of Armenians within Russia. Armenia was an independent country before becoming part of the Soviet Union. Many Armenians wanted to reclaim their independence, but the Soviet Union would not allow them to. This caused tension between the Soviet government and the Armenians. Russians often treated Armenians unfairly. In 1990, Armenia finally regained its independence. Galina Starovoitova's actions helped make this happen.

Galina followed her own advice. She lived simply and did not allow money to corrupt her. She never let politics' demands drive her off course.

At the end of Galina's life, she established an award for people who have helped protect human rights and democracy in Russia. Earning this reward is a great honor, and only a handful of people have ever received it.

Unfortunately, Galina's political enemies were too powerful. Her life ended in 1998, when she was assassinated. She will always be remembered as a brave woman who fought hard for equality and justice. Her legacy reminds us that an anthropologist truly can make a difference, and she is a role model for young women around the world.

Words to Know

Advocate: a person who publicly supports a cause.

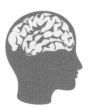

Find Out More

Celebration of Women Anthropologists: "Galina Starovoitova"
anthropology.usf.edu/women/starovoitova/starovoitova.html

Women's Intellectual Contributions: "Galina Starovoitova"
www2.webster.edu/~woolflm/starovoitova.html

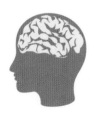

10

Kathy Reichs:

The Real-Life "Bones"

Like the other women in this book, Kathy Reichs found an area of anthropology that interested her most. But hers was quite different from the others'. Kathy's area of expertise became **forensic** anthropology.

Forensic anthropologists study the remains of someone after they have died. Many forensic anthropologists help solve crimes and identify bodies. Like other female scientists before her, Kathy was forced to earn the respect of her colleagues.

Scientists like Kathy are experts in human **anatomy**. They find clues about a person's identity by examining the bones, skin, hair, and **DNA** that was left behind. For example, did you know that you can tell a skeleton's gender just by looking at its **pelvic** bone? You can also determine a body's ethnicity by looking at the skull. Sometimes, a forensic anthropologist is the only person who can solve the mystery of a person's death. The career can be very stressful, but also very rewarding.

Kathy Reichs was born in 1950 and fell in love with science at a young age. She earned her bachelor's degree in anthropology at American University. Kathy then completed her education at Northwestern University, where she eventually received a PhD. She started working with ancient bones but quickly switched over to doing forensic work. Over time, she became an expert at solving crimes. Throughout her career, Kathy Reichs has assisted many organizations, including the FBI! Sometimes, she must appear in court to explain her findings.

Her work has taken her far, but her interests remain the same. What makes Kathy Reichs different from other scientists is her passion for creativity. While other anthropologists simply wrote nonfiction books about their experiences, Kathy found ways to get everyday people interested in forensic science. Although she was well-known for her technical knowledge, Kathy Reichs wrote several novels based on her own life and experience as a forensic anthropologist. This shows that scientists can be both serious and creative! Her first book, *Déjà Dead*, released in 1997, won the Arthur Ellis Award for Best First Novel. Since then, she has released at least a dozen more books. These novels have become so popular that they have been translated into other languages. Each novel serves two purposes. First, it is entertaining, as all novels should be. Second, it is educational. Kathy includes a lot of information about how the main character solves crimes.

More recently, Kathy Reichs also helped produce a popular TV show called *Bones* that premiered on the Fox Network in 2005. The main character of the TV show, Temperance "Bones" Brennan, is named after the main character in Kathy Reichs' novels. Unlike Kathy, Temperance has a much more dramatic life. In 2010, Kathy also published a young adult novel called *Virals*. The main character, Tory Brennan, Bones' niece, uses state-of-the-art forensic science to solve a mystery.

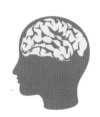

Kathy Reichs at a booksigning. One of Kathy's inspirations for writing is her desire to get people interested in science. A person who reads one of Kathy's novels or watches *Bones* will come away with a lot of knowledge about how a forensic anthropologist does her job. As a female scientist, Kathy also shows us that it is okay to have a creative side. Science does not always have to be completely serious. It can be fun, too!

Kathy has taught at several universities, including Northern Illinois University, University of Pittsburgh, and University of North Carolina at Charlotte. She is married with three grown children. She frequently travels between Canada and the United States, and she has assisted other nations that have asked for her help. Some of these nations include Guatemala and Rwanda. The UN sometimes calls on her for **human rights** work. Kathy proves that when it comes to forensic anthropology, women can do anything!

Words to Know

Forensic: relating to the use of science to solve crimes.

Anatomy: the study of the structure of organisms' bodies.

DNA: deoxyribonucleic acid; a substance passed down from parents to children, and which determines people's individual characteristics.

Pelvic: relating to the region of the pelvis in a living thing's body, located in the area surrounded by the hips.

Human rights: freedoms that all people are entitled to, including food, clean water, and shelter.

Find Out More

ForensicAnthro.com
www.forensicanthro.com

The Guardian. "This Much I Know: Kathy Reichs, Forensic Anthropologist and Writer, 60, London"
www.guardian.co.uk/lifeandstyle/2008/oct/26/1

Kathy Reichs
www.kathyreichs.com

Manhein, Mary H. *The Bone Lady: Life as a Forensic Anthropologist.* New York: Penguin, 2000.

Reichs, Kathy. *Virals.* New York: Razorbill, 2010.

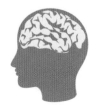

11

Opportunities for Women in Anthropology

Being a female anthropologist hasn't always been easy. Today, women are much more accepted within the scientific community. In fact, they are encouraged to pursue anthropology! Anthropologists understand that women bring a unique perspective to the field.

Field Research

Perhaps one of the most exciting possibilities for an anthropologist is as a field researcher. These anthropologists often travel far and wide in search of answers.

These archeologists are taking measurements for a new dig. Who knows what they will unearth from the ground—and what new information about the people of the past they will discover!

Some anthropologists, known as archaeologists, spend their lives unearthing the mysteries of the past. Much of what we know about ancient civilizations is because of their work. Some anthropologists, however, prefer to interview the living people of different cultures. A female field researcher may have an easier time interviewing women because female anthropologists can identify with the pressures of womanhood, such as giving birth and raising children, better than a man can. Each new study helps us come closer to understanding where humans came from—and where we are headed.

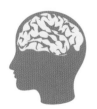

A curator works in places like this one at the University of British Columbia's Museum of Anthropology, best known for its First Nations artifacts. Museums like these help people learn about the cultures of other peoples.

Preservation

All the discoveries made by field researchers need to be documented and preserved by someone. Many ancient artifacts are cataloged and kept in museums to be viewed by the public. A curator is the person who manages the exhibits of a museum. One of the most famous female anthropologists, Margaret Mead, was a curator early in her career. With so many museums around the world, some

female anthropologists are following in her footsteps. Curators often require an anthropological background to ensure that an exhibit is managed properly.

In a way, being an anthropologist is a little like a detective who pays close attention to tiny clues in order to put together a complete picture that will solve a mystery. An anthropologist might help determine the age of various artifacts, for example. She will examine clues, such as what an artifact is made of, how it reacts with certain chemicals, and how it relates to other pieces. Physical anthropologists specialize in the human body and how it has developed. They might spend their time analyzing bones, deciphering a different set of clues.

Teaching and Mentoring

Many anthropologists also teach others. When a cultural anthropologist no longer wants to travel, teaching at a university is the perfect opportunity to pass her knowledge on to the next generation. She will have a lot of stories to tell!

Some anthropologists become **mentors** to young anthropologists who are just entering the field. They may help students with research projects or offer advice on how to get started. Louis Leakey was a mentor to Jane Goodall and Dian Fossey. Franz Boas was a mentor to Ruth Benedict, Margaret Mead, and Zora Neale Hurston. These male mentors were very accepting of female anthropologists at a time where seeing a female scientist was rare. Today, female anthropologists are becoming the mentors of both men and women.

Work in Other Fields

One of the most important qualities of anthropologists is their ability to understand other people. This ability to analyze and understand human beings can be applied to many different fields.

If a company needs someone for **human relations**, it might look for an anthropologist to fill the job. During a criminal investigation, the police may need someone to analyze a criminal's actions, and an anthropologist may be called upon for this task. **Public relations** are another area where some anthropologists excel, especially when it involves negotiating between different ethnicities or cultures.

When it comes to these jobs, it may be easier for a female anthropologist to find her niche. Women tend to be more accepted than men when it comes to

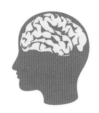

Anthropologists help us imagine the past more accurately, by creating models like this one of ancient Egypt—but they also teach us about different cultures in the world today. They help us understand ourselves better. They show us what it means to be a human being.

the social arena. This is because women have traditionally been considered the more social of the two genders. Of course, this is all changing very quickly as the world learns that both women and men are equally capable.

Teaching at a university . . . consulting with local and international agencies to help fight hunger . . . helping the Census Bureau get accurate counts of homeless people . . . helping an African country merge traditional and Western medical systems . . . teaching a medical center how to provide care to a multicultural community . . . serving as a congressional aide on cultural issues: these are just a few of the many opportunities you might have if you decide to pursue a career in anthropology!

Words to Know

Mentors: experienced and trusted advisors.

Human relations: a department in a company or other organization responsible for hiring new employees, and managing and training current employees.

Public relations: the maintenance of a company's positive image.

Find Out More

American Academy of Forensic Sciences
www.aafs.org/?section_id=resources&page_id=choosing_a_career

American Anthropological Association: "Careers in Anthropology"
www.aaanet.org/profdev/careers

Careers in Archaeology
www.museum.state.il.us/ismdepts/anthro/dlcfaq.html

Careers in Physical Anthropology
www.physanth.org/career/a-career-in-biological-anthropology

Devita, Philip R. *Stumbling Toward the Truth: Anthropologists at Work.* Long Grove, Ill.: Waveland, 2000.

Non-Academic Careers in Anthropology
www.anthropology.pdx.edu/assets/careers.htm

Non-Academic Careers in Physical Anthropology
weber.ucsd.edu/~jmoore/bioanthro/brochure2.html

Stephens, W. Richard. *Careers in Anthropology: What an Anthropology Degree Can Do for You.* Boston: Allyn and Bacon, 2002.

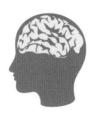

Index

About the Author & Consultant

Shaina Indovino is a writer and illustrator living in Nesconset, New York. She graduated from Binghamton University, where she received degrees in sociology and English. She enjoyed the opportunity to apply both her areas of study to a topic that excites her: women in science. She hopes more young women will follow their calling toward what they truly love, whether it be science related or not.

Ann Lee-Karlon, PhD, is the President of the Association for Women in Science (AWIS) in 2014–2016. AWIS is a national non-profit organization dedicated to advancing women in science, technology, engineering, and mathematics. Dr. Lee-Karlon also serves as Senior Vice President at Genentech, a major biotechnology company focused on discovering and developing medicines for serious diseases such as cancer. Dr. Lee-Karlon holds a BS in Bioengineering from the University of California at Berkeley, an MBA from Stanford University, and a PhD in Bioengineering from the University of California at San Diego, where she was a National Science Foundation Graduate Research Fellow. She completed a postdoctoral fellowship at the University College London as an NSF International Research Fellow. Dr. Lee-Karlon holds several U.S. and international patents in vascular and tissue engineering.

Picture Credits

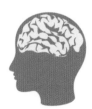